The LORD is My Shepherd

Psalm 23

Picture Book and *Coloring Book*

Illustrated by Josie Blocher

Also by Josie Blocher:
The Thank You Jesus Book - a story book and coloring book combined into one special book.
The Little Tree A Christmas Story
The Little Tree A Christmas Story Coloring Book
God's Wondeful World Story and Coloring Book
I Wonder...? Story and Coloring Book
The LORD is My Shepherd Psalm 23 Picture Book and Coloring Book
The I Am Devotional Coloring Book for women
Answered Prayer, autobiography. Published by Westbow.
Josie Blocher is the author of a 12-part devotional series Diary of the Heart. Volumes 1,2 & *3*
Eternal Streams, Desert Blooms, and *God Bless This Home* are available now.

visit www.josieblocher.wordpress.com

RABBONI BOOK PUBLISHING COMPANY

DEDICATED TO

"...Our Lord Jesus, that great shepherd of the sheep..."

Hebrews 13:20

The LORD is my shepherd;

I shall not want.

He maketh me to lie down
in green pastures:

he leadeth me beside the still waters.

He restoreth my soul:

he leadeth me in the paths
of righteousness
for his name's sake

Yea, though I walk through the valley
of the shadow of death,

I will fear no evil;
for thou art with me;

thy rod and thy staff they comfort me.

Thou preparest a table before me in the presence of mine enemies:

thou anointest my head with oil;

my cup runneth over.

Surely goodness and mercy shall follow me all the days of my life:

and I will dwell in the house
of the LORD forever.

Psalm 23

The LORD is my shepherd; I shall not want.

He maketh me to lie down in green pastures: he leadeth me beside the still waters.

He restoreth my soul: he leadeth me in the paths of righteousness for his name's sake.

Yea, though I walk through the valley of the shadow of death, I will fear no evil: for thou art with me; thy rod and thy staff they comfort me.

Thou preparest a table before me in the presence of mine enemies: thou anointest my head with oil; my cup runneth over.

Surely goodness and mercy shall follow me all the days of my life: and I will dwell in the house of the LORD for ever.

Books for Children

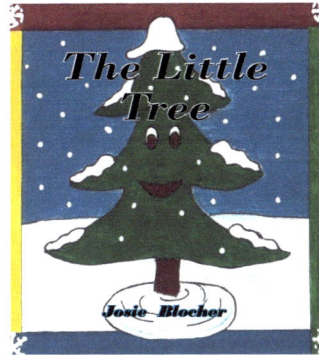

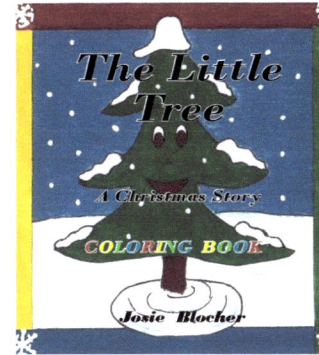

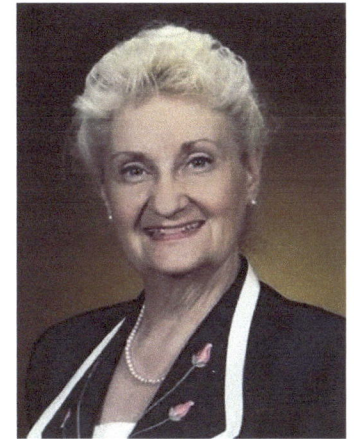

The Little Tree

The Little Tree
A Christmas Story
COLORING BOOK
Josie Blocher

I Wonder...?
Story and Coloring Book
Josie Blocher

THE THANK YOU JESUS BOOK
AND COLORING BOOK
JOSIE BLOCHER

God's Wonderful World
Story and Coloring Book
Josie Blocher

Josie Blocher
Author, Poet
and Artist

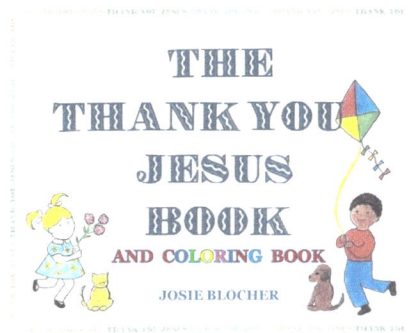

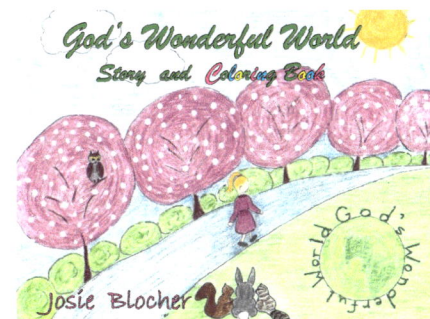

Books for Women

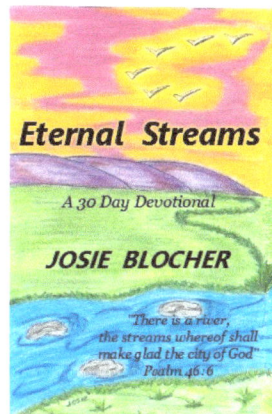

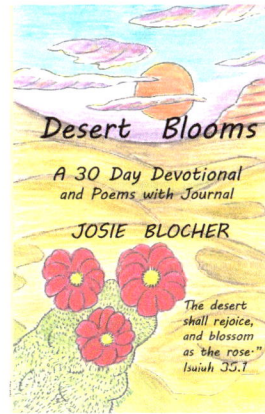

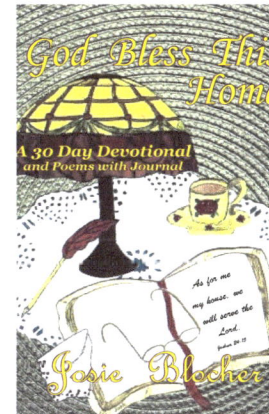

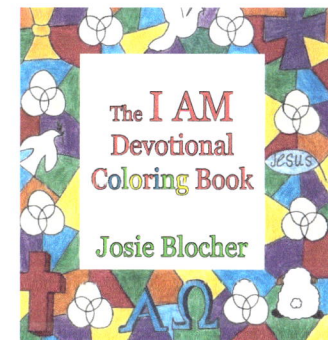

Eternal Streams
A 30 Day Devotional
JOSIE BLOCHER
"There is a river,
the streams whereof shall
make glad the city of God"
Psalm 46:6

Desert Blooms
A 30 Day Devotional
and Poems with Journal
JOSIE BLOCHER
The desert
shall rejoice,
and blossom
as the rose."
Isaiah 35:1

God Bless This Home
A 30 Day Devotional
and Poems with Journal
As for me
my house, we
will serve the
Lord.
Josie Blocher

The I AM
Devotional
Coloring Book
JESUS
Josie Blocher

Other books by Josie available from online and local book retailers